NIGGER

by

LABI SIFFRE

First published in 1993
by Xavier Books
P.O. Box 17 Abergavenny Gwent NP8 1XA

Designed by Mikeith Design
39 Charles Street
Cardiff CF1 4EB

Printed in Great Britain by
Hammetts, Taunton
All rights reserved

© Labi Siffre, 1993
This book is sold subject to the condition that it shall not, by way of trade or otherwise, be lent, resold, hired out or otherwise circulated without the publisher's prior consent in any form of binding or cover other than that in which it is published and without a similar condition including this condition being imposed on the subsequent purchaser.

ISBN 0-9520942-0-7

HUMBERSIDE LIBRARIES
Group BEE
Class 821.914
ISBN
ALS No. 38110661.2

Some of these poems appeared in the limited edition
collection *Positive Images*
Martello Mouse was previously published in
Poetry Wales
A Bridge To Pa was previously published in the
anthology *Black Harvest*

Management by Dave Margereson & Kenny Thomson
for
Mismanagement
754 Fulham Road London SW6 5SH

A *Xavier* Book

Dedicated to PJCL as always

and to the memory of JMBS

CONTENTS

MAN MADE
Creation Myth Also *1*
Ggoderel *2*
Positive Images *3*
Creation Myth Too *7*
New Boy On The Cross *8*
Top O' The World Ma *10*
Prometheus Thinks Twice *11*
Sand:2000 - Rock:Nil *12*
Juju *14*
Lawyer *15*

SENSE
28 Times Fable *16*
Niggers *17*
The 2nd Of 2 Reasons *19*
About *20*
Word Play *22*
In At The Birth Of A Literary Journal-Cardiff June 1992 .... *23*
In Excelsis Pro Tem *25*
He Was Insulted *26*

THE ARTIST
Sacred Waters *27*
Snake Oil *28*
Élite Simulations *29*
Don't Flatter Yourself *30*
Street Cred *32*
Slip O' The Tongue *33*
Reflexion *34*

SAVAGES
Theology Lied *36*
Somewhere In The Jungle *37*
Cutlery *39*
Too Many Second Sons *42*
Bog *44*
The Fashion Conscious *45*
Martello Mouse *46*

FOR LOVE
Manifesto *48*
A Warming *49*
For J.M.B.S. *50*

Living Without Faith Requires More Courage *52*
Reprieve *53*
Gi'me *54*
The Art Of Conversation *55*

PERSUASION
Rheum *56*
When In Rome....We Eat Each Other *57*
Soapbox *59*
I Hate Flies *60*
Another New Jerusalem ,,,,,,,,,,,, *61*
A Bigger Lie *62*
If You Know What's Good For You *63*
Un-Titled *64*
Leisure *65*
Gung-ho *66*
R.S.V.P. *67*

POSITIVELY YOKO
Legs *68*
Apostrophe *69*
The Warrior *71*
Language *72*
Letter to CB *74*
En Passant *76*
Soon *77*

REJOICE
Mickey Mouse *78*
Averse To Archaidia *79*
Blockbuster 2 .... *80*
The Painter The Patron Two Views From The Front *83*

MOVIN' ON
Shaving Mirror Poem *84*
Snap. Shots. *85*
The Adventurers *87*
They've Built A Bypass Around Damascus *89*
The Extremist *91*
A Bridge To Pa *92*

MAN MADE

CREATION MYTH ALSO

We the product
Of God jerking off
Into the dark, silk, kerchief
still
consider ourselves
The Centre

Listen.
Do you hear?
In the empty
distant, a voice
Laughing

GGODEREL

Life is illusion
                  How can you tell

Truth is opinion
                  Maybe

Morals are fashion
                  Yes indeed

A grown up...
                  ...is still a baby

God is alive!
                  It's possible

God is a lie!
                  The same

God is the reason
                  to be cruel

Again and again and again my friend
Again and again and again

POSITIVE IMAGES

        Have you noticed
            how

                    the most
                    important
                    part

           of
        christianity

                    after the church that is...

    you know ?.....

                    jesus ...?

    is never depicted
        as being...
.... well...

                    jewish....

           As
          near
          as one
          can see

        he seems
      to have been

a scandinavian
　candinavian
　andinavian
　ndinavian
　dinavian
　inavian
　navian
　avian
　vian
　ian
　an
　n

　　　　　　　a kind of

　　　　　　　bjorn again christ

And
have you no
ticed how gall
ing it must have
been for the christian
            herr
            hitler
(the archetypal
   aryan beauty)

to have known that
jesus
       probably
       looked
       more
       like
him
than for example...

                paul newman

                'though
                of course
                he didn't
                know
                paul
       personally

and by the way
where are
the other five million of 'em
                hiding

And have
you noticed
how
now that we can hate
         the jews

for being
"like
the nazis"
         it's so much
           easier
         to excuse
           our
         previous
nasties;

and
by
the way

  I just heard someone say

    "This

  is *another* fine mess

    they

    got *us*

    into"

CREATION MYTH TOO

Stale sweat   smell   dead skin

Careless   God steps from the bath

Our journey begins

New Boy On The Cross

"People need something to believe in", he said,
closing the book, bolting the gates
as if this need was of itself
something to be proud of

Abused so, hope took to the bottle;
a futile gesture, correction fluid being no match
for this sword of fire

Men and women reflex crossed their legs
acknowledged impotence outstripped
by this casual castration. It was time
to hie me to the golf course, the snug,
over-coloured prints of persian kittens
Time for the after dinner nap, head pillowed
on that soft pile of skulls
conveniently placed at the camp gates
(You can run
but if you want to hide: stand still)

His compassionate touch drew blood,
"You *will* be saved."
I shook him off: Endure the pain
but not that pleasure.

We circled stationary probing
weighed the dispositions of our forces
stratagems terrain papers moved words
caution betrayed me, he struck

Thrust:
'Cause you don't understand
You think it's rubbish

Parry:
I understand very well
And I think it's crap

Lunge:
'Cause you don't understand
You laugh
When you should be amazed

Counter:
I *am* amazed,
by the way you make a fetish
of self-deception
Where's your self-respect?

À la tête:
What you call self-respect
is vanity and pride
urging you to destroy my faith.

Esquivé:
What you call faith
is intellectual laziness.
You say you know
So how can it be faith?

Poussée:
It is a faith
which has civilised the world
Would you have us return to barbarism?

Riposte:
Your honour
I rest my case

Coup de grâce:
If you really understood
You'd agree with me

?!!*!?!*!!

TOP O' THE WORLD MA

distracted by
the hurt
Inri ality was just
a slip of the son

but ignorance
is no defence
in law

and parents
rarely
listen
to their children

PROMETHEUS THINKS TWICE

At the entrance
to un-manned territory
I Prometheus
hesitate

loath to display
with every step
the depth
of God's
dishonesty

SAND:2000 - ROCK:NIL

In Limbo
bordering on Hell
the just who died before Christ's coming dwell
As do benighted babies lacking
words and H_2O baptismal

Twice denied (the rite
and then the light of heavenly beams)
it seems a shabby way to greet
the worthy and the innocent
of even the most trivial
of venial misdemeanours.

To the troglobytes of our golden age
of actuarial jurisprudence
it may seem injudicious
some might even venture "rash"
to be so previously born

The hordes of decent, upright, honest,
ordinary, working men and women
in their low rise BC homes
on their busy BC streets
should, with common sense and forethought
(and professional consultation)
have withstood or neutralised
the brushed green baize effect
where faith, roulette, and loaded dice
divinely intersect

Je ne regrette rien
Perhaps the Magister's a Piaf fan

So babes, like those Great Herod killed,
'though far too young to know "free will"
to lust, to fornicate, to swill,
making the most of things for ages
autobiographies with pristine pages
are juggling tons of vacuum and less
(exacting in the void with nothing to confess)

Their's not to reason why
Their's but to do the decent thing
and love the lie.

JUJU

Me Dad believed in Juju
as the Pope does
(to be fair
I think the Pope would call it
The Power of Prayer)

Me Dad believed in Juju
so he sent us to the priests
And they believe it's who you know
so the least was said
'bout Galileo

Me Dad believed in Juju
potions, dolls, witch-doctors rites
The priests believe in Virgin Birth
the blood and wine of Christ

Me Dad believed in Juju
I believe it may be so
Anything is possible
I doubt we'll ever know

When the dead rise up
On judgement day
For God's sake
He'd better have a good lawyer

SENSE

28 TIMES FABLE

Mouthing
a semblance of concern
for the world's well-being

they wear, as a badge of courage,
ignorance
bastioned by
The Certain Belief

that delicate declension
of righteousness

NIGGERS

                        We don't need Niggers

                                anymore

                We got something even better

                            Every colour

                                can abhor;

                Most abuse is in the family

                              (convenient

                                to ignore);

                      Thank God for Gays

                      We don't need Niggers

                              anymore

                    We don't need Niggers

                              anymore

                    We found something

                              even better

What we've all

been searching for;

With a scapegoat

you can boost your ego

(that's how humans

score);

Thank God for Gays

We don't need Niggers

anymore

THE 2nd OF 2 REASONS

As you know
The overwhelming
majority of people in the world
with HIV or AIDS
are heterosexual

It's been that way (in the real world)
right from the start
but most of them aren't
white
which makes them not quite
human enough
                    to interest our media,
the Pope, chief Rabbis, Archbishops,
Prime Ministers or Presidents
(in or out of the gutter)

and for the past few years
the word "decency"
has made me want to vomit

ABOUT

I doodle advice and eye
contact
Admire and applaudingly yes
your motives   and no to deflect
but default to the serious
Pitfalls awaiting heroes about
to come out
to their strai(gh)t friends.

Framed in the frieze
around this cool of insight, the light
breathes self-consciously
tracing a vision of you and the woman
who says, "I *do* understand", and accepts you
(as one of the girls)   in depth discussions
on recipes, fashion, interior design,
and everyone kisses the air these days.

Turning the shave in the nicotine bar
they'd been playing the game in suits
of "hard but fair"
Punishing down the beer and motoring
shoulder to shoulder in technical specifications
before sauntering home to the strife
and shoving it in (or so
they'd tell each other, and you)

But now the bravo is camping it up
displaying a talent for this in excess
of your own by far   Camping it up
believing that that is how you

naturally behave   that is,
When you're not with the men,
Pretending.

I suppose it's their way
of trying to maintain
the sun in its orbit
around the earth
But I've had to break off several
friendships with straights
because of this kind of thing

It's sad
foolish
patronising
prejudiced

I know

but I just can't help it.

WORD PLAY

What the hell do they mean
by "Lifestyle" and "Preference"

Sexuality is
What you are (no choice)
not something you change
with the Paris
fashions

"Sexual Lifestyle"
and "Sexual Preference"
are phrases honest
as "Ethnic Cleansing"

and the three are used
by similar people
for similar reasons
to similar   effect

IN AT THE BIRTH OF A LITERARY JOURNAL
CARDIFF JUNE 1992

"Two men having sex is obscene."
He explained
He wouldn't have that in his magazine.

The editor/poet in swaddling clothes
had replied to an earlier question,
"I know what's obscene."
From behind my beer I'd inserted,
"Well that scares the shit outa me."

"Homosexuality is wrong", he said.
"Well, I'm gay", I said, "but what if it was
a brilliant poem,
Would you publish it in your magazine?"

"Two women having sex would be fine",
he smiled,
"I like that", he smiled again, "I'd put that in."
I said, "Hmmn,

but what if it was, as I've said,
a brilliant poem about two men having sex,
would you publish it in your magazine?"

Without anaesthetic   the pain
was extreme:
He said,
"Yes.   Alright.   I'd allow that."

23

It was then that I wanted to hit him,
kill him? But killing him would have been like
killing one locust in a swarm:
gratuitous.

Instead
I went home
Lay down by your side
And our two men shadows
In the full moon light
Made perfect
Sense

IN EXCELSIS PRO TEM

Egelantier
In exchange for my crude billet doux
tie me to this, the key, if not to love,
then to parole substantial enough
to permit the seeking heart
to fill in the forms
while faded officials bolster
imagined superiority
with my hesitant biro

Egelantier
comfort me not with certainty,
the light by which the foolish maidens
see nothing but themselves;
Speeding home in their Father's stolen car
aware, vaguely, feeling the bumps, thud
hearing the cries of the maimed:
the surprise of the deleted
the flesh strewn highway
to be dismissed later
as over-reaction

Egelantier
comfort me with a vision
of uncivilised H_2O
dry stone walls on the road to damask napkins
and the postponement of a healthier diet;
and when (finally?) I bid you goodnight,
leaving these engravings,
let me believe in this first step
and this first step
and this
and this and this

Egelantier: A gay bathouse in Amsterdam.

HE WAS INSULTED:

that another man

could find him

attractive

Ashamed:

to think

there must be signs

effeminate

about him

Pathetic:

needing to believe

that men
who sex to men
not women

nonetheless

seek women

in their men.

THE ARTIST

These waters are sacred
to those who do not know their name;
no matter
we are ever strangers here
and words
merely an arrangement
of misunderstandings

SNAKE OIL

His poems never drew blood
or teeth
They never thrashed, blasphemed
or screamed at impotence   or shed
defenceless tears   or skin
or made a weapon clenched for battering
No punching holes in prison walls   his knuckles
were intact   reserved
for making sure of still births
and infanticides

His poems never vomited
or farted, wanked or raped
or sucked indifference to a gasping
submission
Those who championed his work admired how
'though he used obscenities
his poems never swore
His publishers admired this talent most of all

And in a land that boasted of it's poets
but had little time for poetry,
he awoke each morning   stressed steel
cock erect   and aching to maintain
the sacramental dream
Unable to remember
if there'd been one

ÉLITE SIMULATIONS

The élite
    saw Joy
on the gallery wall
and said *Yes*
But what does it mean?

The élite
    saw Love
on the gallery wall
and most of them
thought it obscene

The élite
    saw Death
on the gallery wall
and said *Yes*
But why make it so sad?

The élite
    saw Cash
on the gallery wall
and were grateful
for the deeply
moving
experience
that they'd had

DON'T FLATTER YOURSELF

you tell me I write for you
you tell me I'm trying
to reach you you tell me I'm trying
to tell you something
you tell me that that is offensive

you tell me the way to say
something
is to say
nothing
that trying to say something
is self
(defeating)
I say only you can see with your eyes
(you offer remedial glasses)

you tell me the way to be true to oneself
is not to try
I tell you I'm trying not to
you tell me the way to be free
is to be as nothing
I tell you that most of us have succeeded
you tell me my attitude is élitist
I tell you to go to hell
you tell me to lighten up
to trust my instincts
you tell me to Go With My Feelings!

Amen!

Cleansed by your philosophy I, liberated,
Knock you to the ground

you threaten litigation
I, encouraged to encourage the real me, refuse
to apologise
and grasping an almost empty bottle of the market
leader in a popular indifference
smash it to your temple
breaking a vaginal path for the spread red sea

And we are not alone:
the shoal of customers light silvered eyes
flashing as one to our fierce choreography
measure your progress through pain, shock and anger as I,
helpless weak with the virus of living
(the need to be loved)
have no choice but to give the audience what it wants:

and as you gather your feet
I headbutt you square in the mouth
breaking teeth
which you swallow, they catch in the snatch
of your throat
you deflate, gargling blood, yet
cry out with a critical choke
that the concept of changing the world with my scribbles
is gauche!

I agree
suggesting you cast that idea from your mind as, as
a wilderness youth many years ago
I did.

STREET CRED

i ain't never been a steel worker
                              a miner
or a soldier
(the killing kind it'd have to be:
don't count if you ain't never killed nobody)

i ain't never run with a street gang
or rolled a drunk (though i screwed a few)
an' I ain't never been a sharecropper
or a jack hammer, dirty white, pick-axe shovelling vest

i ain't never been inside or died
been on the road or muscle at the dock side
with a few beers more to make it on home
for the best of three falls   to defend the title
an' break her balls before she breaks mine
man

i ain't never done horse
or been divorced
been or pounded rock
needed de-tox
stole a car once, cream shit that don't count
(didn't get caught)
an' i ain't never screwed a hooker
'though i worked for a few
been screwed by 'em too
an' i ain't been to vegas
so wha' do i do:

What have I got
to write about?

SLIP O' THE TONGUE
(For Salman Rushdie, and many others)

Words are not free, Gillian.

You forget
so many places
where life is cheap
and words
offending the weak (so easily
the strongest of us all) so
easily remove   Colossus
(the strong enough to speak).

I missed out
not seeing Hendrix
"live"
but I did see
Stephen Spender.
        He said
he was suspicious
of political poetry;
        I liked him
But is there
any other kind?

When all the poets
are jailers
And the jailers
laureate
The sermon on the mount
is just another picnic.

Words are *not* free, Gillian.
But you know that
really
Don't you?

REFLEXION

It's
the dishonesty
I despise in hare coursing
You can't trap life in a field
of arrogant cowardice set your servants
to ripping it to rags then claim the day
with a lie bigger than a bullfight Life
is at the track giving the hounds
the finger ever out of reach
and anyway your chasing
a fake.

Like the dressing
room I'd been too busy to shit
and with toxic towels de-composing
memories of caffeine blight
glazing the remains
of an all night
cancer party
we were
full of
it

But I got ready
ready to rehearse ready
to get ready to do the show
for people who perform most of
their lives and think *I'm* acting

So we did two run throughs and I was good
you could tell by the way the crew
knew why they were,   smiled
and the hangers
quit phasing

and
I heard
safety leaving
the stage so I followed
thinking good I can shit now
and I did next door to the dressing
room in the wide open space of
a toilet for the disabled

and
I got
rid of what
I'd enjoyed the day
before and I wiped and I
re-aligned and I douched the digits
and I stepped out in front of a waiting
Wheelie and he said, "What the fuck do you think
you're doing in there!?! You're not disabled!!"
And I looked him in the anger and I said
"Yeah well maybe the crutches don't
show" and he said "Bullshit!"
And he was right
I guess

SAVAGES

Theology lied

The soul is on the outside

in society

Somewhere in the jungle
Tarzan is swinging to the rescue
but for the moment
Jane and Boy are in grave peril.

High up in the canopy
Tarzan has sex on his mind;
Can't wait to get home
and throw Jane into the river.

He practises his credit card
vocabulary quick and easy to use,
Suitable for any commanding occasion;
animals, natives (every species)
accurately respond to "Ngowa!...Ngowa!"

The escarpment almost magnificent as he,
The jungle lord pauses to survey his domain;
Oh why is Jane still not pregnant?
Perhaps they're not swimming often enough.

Back at the tree-house, Boy is fighting
for justice, truth and the arboreal way
against the evil leopard men
and their throat ripping, metal talons.

Jane, his adoptive jungle mother, helps
by standing in the corner, poised,
the back of her hand to her lovely mouth,
eyes fixed wide with horror.

Strange how pale these natives look
Mexican or Mediterranean in style;
There is obviously a shortage of Negroes
on the dark continent.

When he lands, Tarzan find's Paradise In Disarray;
No sign of his cub or Mate; only Cheeta,
at home on the dining room table
doing "Cheeta like" things with Jane's lipstick.

CUTLERY

In marsupial pocket
in a small aspirin bottle
My father would carry
dilute disinfectant

My brother, my mother and I he'd embarrass
by cleaning, publicly,
restaurant cutlery;
How could I hide at a moment like that
'cept by feigning indifference
studying, casually,
fellow sophisticates
Cool
Well you had to be:

Eight years old at bay:

The whole school laughed
When the White Father told us
and showed us with slides and demean Amen
How the natives in Africa needed our help
How they didn't know God and His laws Unh Unh
How they lived in mud huts Ha Ha
Ate roast monkey Hee Hee
With grub sauce Ugh Ugh:
How our duty it was then
to save them.

It seemed as if everyone laughed except me
I recognised something in those on the screen
And afterwards, some of the other boys asked me
'cause I was the only black boy they knew

What was it like in my mud hut Ha Ha
Eating roast monkey Hee Hee
With grub sauce Ugh Ugh
I beat two of them up
Then they left me alone
No, it wasn't enough.

I went home and tried desperately
scrubbing the black from my body
discovering blood.

"Are you white underneath"
the white boys would play
" Let me feel your hair
It's like wool !"
To this day I can't stand to have anyone touch my hair
"Is your Willie black too?!"

They seemed to believe that one chose to be black
Like today they believe people choose to be gay
That's different they say
and still they believe
We could all be white
if we *really* tried.

Eight years old at bay:

With luck, other customers, wandering waiters
had been blind to my fathers obsession with germs
(At home, after smiling, waving good-bye
and locking the door
he would wash all the doorknobs
that might have been touched
by visiting friends or relations).

My mother, my brother and I relaxed.
The ritual over. Survived.
Our food arrived.

My father, my mother, my brother and I
took up our spoons and our forks and began
Pork sweet and sour with chicken chow mein
crispy noodles and special fried rice
And that's when I got my surprise:
Across the way
A brand new game to play:

The women and men who discovered America
"Red Indians"
Who gave a damn about them?
So I think *I'll* lay claim
to discovering....the chopstick....

'Til I'd seen one
I'd n'ere ever seen one
'Til then.

TOO MANY SECOND SONS

With their savagery
they startled baboons
in places where galleried genius
will be forever gauche
unless conceit

Valiant in extremis
when threatened with mango,
witchetty, banyan, maize,
They prevailed
adept with flame throwers

In silica sanctums
market gardens
freezer centres and fish tanks
subtle commerce
far beyond the brawling of the Bourse
was categorised as sterile:
defile
attack
bury
or stack
denial
pack
and forget.

The remaindered memories
hinterlanded shadows pressed
in tattered consequences
creatures without

faces
fire-hungry
gathering hate
the warmth that chills

Each one consumes
an ash cake
bile binding a dead vocabulary

These ceremonies seem endless

Cragfast
Others begin

On a wall
In the bog
At "The Four Bars
Inn" an angry tone
"ENGLISH GO HOME"
Which from my point of view
was refreshingly new

Now that I live in Wales, it's nice to be told to "piss off" because I'm English.

The fashion conscious
breathed a sigh of relief

when Nelson Mandela
was released.

"Apartheid's dead", they laughed
"We can all go home".

"It's business as usual"
the regime intoned

and Apartheid still bleaches white
Young black bones

MARTELLO MOUSE

I was climbing the stairs
in the junior school
when someone descending
(I don't know who)
casually gave me
the present that stayed with me
that day to this
no wrapping no kiss
no brotherly hug
and none of his love
no box and no card
just the label
"Black Bastard"

Thirty years on
when my father heard death
in the garden
weeding
decided to marry
my mother
her joy was the message
a phantom remission
this humming bird flight

To protect
I reflected electric delight
the pro from my Hollywood
home without home
but the Martello Mouse
was a miner,
regret,
The gift horse to Troy, a brick
from my lesion built wall

See, 'til then
when the warrior, might
in his armour of speeding car,
heavy mates, distance, drew
that dagger to flay the affront
my existence
my existence grew
as my smile broke through
and I'd think, "You prat,
If you only knew".

FOR LOVE

MANIFESTO

I will wait
for you

Knowing even
that we will never meet again

I will wait
for you

A WARMING in my (now our)
bed
You brought me
sight
denied
by tungsten

YOU SLEEPING tigers breath
on my sparse haired chest
Sum total of my
happiness

IN SHADOW
parts of you you
never see
Intimately precious
to my memory
and me

FAMILIARITY BREEDS
a lack of attention.
Twenty eight years on, you
fascinate me still.
Have we been
perfect
strangers?

FOR J.M.B.S.

Remember
that first illicit night
      we agreed
    about our total
incompatibility
while falling indelibly
in love

Remember we needed
to decide who would be first
           to give in
so we both did

Remember you were four
and I was twelve;
'though you so much the elder
             touching
I was older still

Remember how
no breath to be afraid
you learned to play my games
We won so many in that single bed
               we overlapped
and cried inside relief
and understanding found such honesty
our natural belief.

Remember how
new-found we lay
(I feel your furnace now)
sometimes you'd read me Robbie Burns

                    I hardly understood
but understood you very well and kissed
the sense of you
from foot   to head
and back   to taste
myself   in your mouth

Remember how you died and left me
falling
Just the week before, we'd spent a day
visiting the towers of your business friends
I waiting, patient chauffeur to the shadow in your brain

Remember
how that night I slept beside
You on our slender bed
Me on the floor beneath your breath
Too late the faithful hound
to tear that hid assassin into shreds

Then next day I
driver once again
You to your plane and home to far away
Too far to hold your hand in time
I wrote too late for your reply
Your teasing me, as ever,
on the scarcity of my
inscribed kiss.

LIVING WITHOUT FAITH
REQUIRES MORE COURAGE

Last night I dreamed about you once again
This happens often   six years on
there's been no healing
Am I living out of time?

I dreamed I saw you on the street
Across the road in front of me
Walking with a little dog: beside your heavy bulk
It looked absurd
You didn't have a dog when we were lovers.

One day, looking through your past
I found a photograph of you
aged five or six   my future
front row prop, wary of the lens, unsmiling,
shading your eyes from the seaside sun
Holding the lead of a terrier dog
in your full fleshed clenched left hand.

'Though knowing I was in a dream
I couldn't help
but call your name;
I ran across the road to hold you
You turned around
Then I woke up   and saw
beyond the darkness of my room
another   darker still.

REPRIEVE

When I'm late for a good idea
When I tell my side of the story
but have neither the time
nor the patience
to listen

When I run to catch the last chance
and find myself
on the wrong
conclusion
stranded
hunched against the cold way home

Disparate I rummage
and smile
finding your love
in my pocket

GI'ME

Gi'me a bite of your apple
Gi'me a slice of your life
Gi'me a place on your planet
At least
        let me keep you in sight

Gi'me a chance at your window
Let me be your point of view
And when you tire of talking
Let me be something to do

Let me be part of your make-up
Ever caressing your skin
Let me be there when you wake up
Open your door
Let me in

THE ART OF CONVERSATION

Hearing the poet
Bemoaning the banality
Of the language of love

Made me think of us
Making 69
and speaking

Magic
With our mouths
Full

PERSUASION

RHEUM

Perhaps the winning politicians place

is merely to display the outward signs

of our inner disgrace

WHEN IN ROME...WE EAT EACH OTHER

Visible from the moon
we remain
The Great Wall of China
Spraying ourselves with slogans   loudly
denouncing betrayal in basic black   resolutely
without pearls   inflammatory red smoke
without fire:
Some things, at least, are going according to plan.

Yet, try as we might,
and we do (observing a subtle but stifling dress code)
it's hard to ignore the photos
                addresses
                dates
and our own signed affidavits plastered cold
to the backs of our eyes.

Tying the knot has become *à la mode*
as comfort stations close all over the land.
"You're the five thousand and fifty third one today.
I keep telling 'em, 'There's just no call for it' ".

We press our knees and tightly thighs together
clutch ourselves in desperandum as the big boys
piss on our faces   and we agree   responsibility
weighs heavy on their bladders.

No, they have not bought us with false coin.
We recognised the scam and loved it
lapping it up in our warm, wet,
child-bearing mouths.

And had we not known?
Well, we should have.
We've seen the same embossed gloss
timeless times before   The same sign
loudly ringing on the palace door:
"Something For Hardly Anything At All".

But have no fear
We'll be allowed, *no, encouraged,*
to go, gentle, into that good night,
the children, wise, not cursing our behaviour

Craven as we   they realise
they will soon stand
exactly
where we are standing now.

SOAPBOX

>Don't lecture me man
>That's no way to be changing me
>I know didacticism
>Hell, I live it

>So just sidle on up to me
>Subtle and sly
>That's the way to persuade
>And in the mean time

>Gimme your watch
>And your wallet
>Then get down on your knees
>And *suck my future*

Gently now
Gently
>The last thing we want
>is a revolution

I hate flies
really hate 'em
loathe their filthy, disease carrying habits

tasting your food with their feet
vomiting
then sucking the vomit back up
with some of your food
mixed in
I kill 'em whenever I can

sprays, supplements, rolled up newspapers,
paperback latest sci-fi thriller
but a hand-towel is best
and for distance track-suit
bottoms held by the ankles

and now you say
they pollinate more flowers than bees do
THWACK!!

That's something I'll have to
think about

ANOTHER NEW JERUSALEM

Eyes bright
Shorn of confusion
We are The New Breed
Practical, pragmatic, pledged
To this vital reclamation of our land;

And it is with results, not words,
That we confirm our purpose;
Observe us, retracing and retracing our steps
Filling the craters and chasms
With the bodies of our dead

A BIGGER LIE
(After Paul Joseph Goebbels)

Democracy doesn't mean freedom

When the majority vote to outlaw free speech
democracy *has* been served

Marketing rules in democracies
and those who want freedom
to hold sway
had best make it seem more attractive
and less
of a threat to the vain, the cowards, the weak:

It's the powerful you have to persuade.

IF YOU KNOW WHAT'S GOOD FOR YOU

Little man don't waste your time with big
questions
The world is ruled by giants
Men so powerful
so different to your kind they are
Tigers to your single celled
embarrassment

Little man best leave important questioning
to them
as they possess the planet with their many-
headed, mouthed and stomached harvesters
onward into space, triumphant, mindful
of their divine right
and the universe's sell by date

Little man beneath them
do you not feel foolish scurrying
among the jungled stalks of knowledge
life and death decisions
with your broken scissors

Little man confine your laboured self
to entertainment
After all, it's tough enough just getting by;
be "satisfied survivor" little man-
content
The conscience of the tasty deer
won't halt the hungry tiger

UN-TITLED

Indeed an end to division

When the honourable men agree

To name dishonesty

"Pragmatism"

LEISURE DEVELOPMENT

RAVISHING SCENERY

GUNG-HO

>Blood on your hands
Lo, pronounce to the world
that the world is unbearably full
and the mother whose bundle of joy you've delivered
would rather "Congrats! It's a girl!"
so you'll have to be
doctor be, patient be
wait for the hole in the sky
for the glow from the sea
saw the mote in the eye
was the right to confound
with a troop of one's own
the plane we *don't* own
the right to be crushed, to be crowded
to savour the taste of the smell of the zoo
How d'ya do to the stranger who's smelling for you
on the eight-fifteen, on the five forty-two
It's a hell of a job but a man's gotta do
what a man's gotta do
and a woman too

R. S. V. P.

Understanding is impossible
Acceptance   that
we will never understand
is beyond our understanding

In the forest, the tree falls
We see furniture

On the table, the harvest fails
We see prices

Bereaved, the un-heard world mourns
over a full belly of fear

The balconies are swollen with marauders
extolling the virtues of a peace
they *will not* afford

And the runways of the world
awash with saliva
lead us to the lavender smell
of children for sale

While the doctor, history,
struggles to read his own writing,
the patient is terminal
at birth
the spark so brief
the poet is hard
pressed to realise
even the first line

POSITIVELY YOKO

**THINGS SHE MEANT TO SAY
BUT THOUGHT OF TOO LATE (Part 1)**

"It may be
a matter of exhaustion
but I can't seem to get
my legs
around your impertinence."

APOSTROPHE

Tactfully
she believes
in every word he says
while making
ever more frequent
visits
to the bathroom

Leafing through
his suggestions
blank pages
cages
for spontaneity
intuition
wit
whine by whine
the marshmallow grows fangs

A frayed
she rails against his lack
of insight.   Nature, faith,
science, superstition: wasted.
Surely there's...
Don't say surely!
Surely means you're not.
But
certainly
there's no better time than now
to be profound,
with Charon, eager,
rapping his staff
on this unyielding shore.

She studies her
Optometrist's report
for hint of some perhaps genetic,
get out/justification/excuse
for her own lack of insight
After all, this vacuum is nothing new
Why has she, 'til now, not noticed?

Kisses congeal on his chimney breast
She comforts the lover
who comforts the lover
who etc.,
and as the worm turns
beneath her breath
beneath his skin
beneath his flesh
she views the future all too clearly
and fucks her way to sanctuary
taking refuge in nostalgia in advance
each thrust a memory that will not last

"We are fighting for freedom", the warrior said.

"We will fight for our freedom until we are dead".

"Unlock our chains", cried the women he met.

"Of course", smiled the warrior,

"But not just yet".

LANGUAGE

(1)

Just this evening
Determined to avoid a night on the down
She gives him pause for nought

"You lust be joking", she says,
"We speak completely different tokens of our affectations.
From our national inclinations we must break free
You, from New Talk (say more, feel less)
Me, from Begin (silent witness
to the trend of civilisation as we blow it)".

"Don't I know it", he says, looking deep into her eyes,
"You're absolutely right
I understand, I really do,
I sympathise with your point of view
Can we go to bed now?"

(2)

Several times a week
Between her thighs
He flies

                    Several times a week
                    Between her thighs She
                                    lies

Several times
A weak between her thighs
He trembles

                    Several times
           a weak between her thighs
                                she
                    Dissembles

Several times a week, between her sighs,
She considers how, in the land of the blind,
The one eyed man is at best
confined
The one eyed woman ignored
or reminded
to wait.

(3)

Just this evening
Determined to avoid
A night on the down
He refuses to acknowledge her grief
To turn the sound of his voice
to relevant intimations

Instead, he sends
Insultingly   Patronising
Invitations which she
accepts:

Everyone needs to be recognised.

LETTER TO CB

Dear Charles Bukowski
I've loved your poems
from the first I read
three years ago
& yes I know
You don't give a shit
& yes of course
There has to be
a "but"
and here it is:

You've written a lot
about whores as less
unless they're the type who give
then get back in the box; add on fixtures
to men who drink
& drink & gamble & fuck
& drink & gamble & fuck
& write
(men we soft
never jump, safeties,
admire/ envy/ identify with
from a distance)
& that's OK but what
pisses me off
is the lack of a mention
that those of us
who go with whores
are whores.

Well, that's it I guess
except for me to wonder
whether you'll be dead
before my thoughts
arrive

unnoticed
mostly
people flush their lives away
your poems say you didn't
I agree
& 'though you may not care
nor think so at the finish, I
un-still
thank you
in this uphill kind of way

as from a sapling
to a tree

Best wishes

Labi Siffre.

EN PASSANT

        Another thing
    about The Saint Matthew Passion
There's a bit of the text which describes/praises
        the Virgin Mary as/for being
            Undefiled
            you know
            hymen-wise

        Had I been a mother
my clawed tongue would have bloodied the sky
        at this implicit insult
        Mouths spouting that muck
            make fuck a blessing
        But the weak always did despise
            the vision without which
        they'd have no use for eyes

SOON

One day soon
As soon is measured
(by the fornifications of embellished truths)
She will bestir herself
No more deceit   the fear
of more
or less
She's on her feet

One day soon
As soon is measured
(by the abjudications of undeclared interests)
She will be late
Herself no more   'though more
her self
She's at the door

One day soon
As soon is measured
(by the accumulation of inevitable betrayals)
She will berate herself no more
But merely shrug
And leave the room

REJOICE

Sun   fun   and Mickey Mouse

Disneyland in the desert

The gulf between us

AVERSE TO ARCHAIDIA

I am the soldier
Born to bleed
We swear that in the military
We live to kill the thing we love;
Rejoice! The theatre is so vast
The wit of man so small
They may be silent in the circle
But they're dying in the stalls.

I am interned
My walls, rank, smell
of dreams consigning him to hell.
His father's father's distant sires
Divining right as their bitch-born desires
Displaced mine own with acrid peace;
Cast out to play the lesser beast
I kneel to Saviour History
Sweet sacrament revenge I test
between my tempered teeth whereon
his blood a moment quells my rut
And titles me Legitimate.

I am the daughter
I the son
of cities you've both shat upon;
You free us (crying
"liberty!") to frolic, orphans, amputees;
We weary of your play with words
"Peace keeping"   "No surrender"
Further casualties bedeck your boasts unfurled
You are too stupid
to change the world

BLOCKBUSTER 2

went to hay-on-wye today
remembrance day
hadn't bought a poppy
don't go out much.

'though i missed 'em by some years
and then a day or two
the two world wars are special to me
feeling as i do about the right to fight
to choose who's going to tell you what to do.

and there's a piece of news-reel
shows a soldier being shot
and as his only life is leaving in a hurry why
surprise to see
his sincere death is nothing
like as good as in the movie;
just a sack of something loose
and heavy
thlump
without a sound
but very

then before you know, it's just
a small commercial break   some people think
a break is what his soul is taking   maybe so
but this soft sell
will it compel the flow in swelling conurbations?
merchandise well demographically, hmmn?

though precise
black and white is a negative move
and the music is hardly the funkiest groove
and a long shot? well yes, i can see that could work
if he staggered and fell and then
crawled, rose and lurched from screen right the whole width
to screen left, past the church
(sound of bullet on bell).

from an overhead view of his zig-zagging recoil
from shell-bursts and debris and ricochet sounds
to the slow-motion following
all   the way   down
as a boiling inferno consumes atlanta once again
in the background.

à tempo with celli
the mighty has fallen
with brass, bass and drums in accord
as municipal paving receives the applause
of his helmet and head
the fragile succumbs to the swarm of inquisitive lead

and we're begging for close up

you'd have to move in
for the blood
the snot
the fear
the dying

the clutching indifferent earth   fingers torn
very special effects for the guts being born
to the clenching of eyelids
a furrowing tear
making parallel track with the blood from his ear

shallow breathing in three hundred speaker surround
lacking only the stench from surrendering bladder and bowel
we zooom to the bluebottle tasting the ground
where mother, sister, father perhaps
placed remembrance
kisses in an earlier flashback.

Did the boy have a lover
to move to this mouth
where bluebottle children will be dining out?

Did the boy have a lover
to move to this tongue
jackdaws and crows will feed on?

He came 'cause they told him to come
They came to take protein from

He came 'cause they told him to come
We came to see cliché for fun

No failure in cliché
cliché's all there is
and to get bums on seats
the familiar wins every time   signed
in different, indifferent designer clues.

He came 'cause they told him to come
They came to the mirrors
left penniless cups

He came 'cause they told him to come
We came to feel something

but never enough

THE PAINTER THE PATRON
TWO VIEWS FROM THE FRONT

In the office
When your tongue met mine
Embracing the heat of battle
With my hand in your pocket
your hand in my soul
I knew that for lovers   death
is a serious business.

Later   in the garden,
searching for flowers
I faltered   finding only
wet   black   ashes
and brought you this crude
token.

                    Now
          in the heat of battle
            your tongue beating
                against mine
                    I realise
              that for lovers
Business is a serious death.

MOVIN' ON

SHAVING MIRROR POEM

It's comforting to think
I did this
and that
and then moved on
but I probably did this
and that
and stayed here

Snap. Shots.

the first time i saw
my mum take her teeth out
i thought it was wonderful
must have been five
and i tried and i tried
but i couldn't get my teeth
to slippin' and slide out
no way could i capture
the click an' no doubt
as she took her teeth out
the matter o' fact
as she clacked 'er teeth back

•

it's unfair
that i have to wear
his old trunks
un-sleek
unlike any others on this beach
mum-made of maroon
coloured wool waterlogged
heavy with blackpool
couldn't swim if i could
inadequate dignity
one paddle backing
slack elasticity

•

twenty feet up
unassailable
never go back
and they'll never know where
anyway they don't care about me
so i'm staying forever so there
right here in this tree
that'll teach 'em a lesson
for mistreating me
i wonder
if Mum's made a cake
for tea

•

over the hills and far away
to once upon a faerie tale
of fabulous friends in fun pretendings
ever after
happy endings

•

THE ADVENTURERS

Words fall   pioneers
from the pages of her migrant tongue
"You have to be scared to be brave"

Into the potion of silences
between bees and belonging
relief at that and stained glass killers,
dragonflies (no jury would convict).

Past slow, juicy, bump right into you
dung flies she doesn't like at all
she and her words fall
past plane song and bird song
and para-gliding spiders
to the bladed sunfed rain
where they cling   breathing.

"It really is the height of arrogance" he'd said,
"this needing less".

Pre-ordained   sheep with important
appointments to keep but no diaries   think
with their teeth   chewing time   again time
'til time passing on her words to grudging, thin living
soil wherein and out of rhyme poems grow
sufficient to the father   but the boy
doesn't look back
daren't look back

and black Islamic birds cut and slice
and hollow out the blue remembering

nothing of that   or that last moment
or do they?

as below, the buzzard, between cardiac calls,
exchanges threats backwards   tumbling
with an impertinence of jackdaws
who never get too close
(the buzzard can't be sure of that)

and children warm urgent with now
chasing racing wrestling,
her words in bunches
binding them in promise laughing dancing
threatening,
with found poems in their hands and hair

And when it must be   time
and time leaving, as it must be,
her words fall and the voices run home
to watch TV
not noticing, in the bracken
(where there are no questions)
the heart beats of mice and rabbits
sharing their name with the long death
silent   keeping.

and later the dog and the orphaned farmer take
Away the sheep to be killed
and some of the children eat
some of the sheep for dinner
watching the latest thriller
or is it the news remembering
nothing of that   or that last moment
or do they?

"It really is the height of arrogance" he'd said,
"this needing less".

THEY'VE BUILT A BYPASS AROUND DAMASCUS

"I've had it with the naive sixties
What an embarrassment
The liberal seventies
Peace and love was a children's game
betrayed us all with it's self-indulgence

The permissive society
What did that give us
Flares, poppers, and pompous pop singers
lecturing us as if they alone
had discovered compassion

Well where's utopia now?
On a drip
in the AIDS ward.   Meaning:
The dream was a catwalk sham,
an Indian summer of guilt and paisley posturing...

To sighs of relief
we grew up in the eighties
Greed ain't good but at least it's honest
The weak are weak 'cause they like to fall
and the strong have to grab as much as they can
in order to save us all
'Get off the cross! Someone else needs the wood!'
In your cardboard boxes you'd do the same to us
if you could."

So here am I, a poet pressed
to the clear sighted nineties
where taking a positive stance is the answer
as we fight our corner and keep our heads

below the parapet (never giving offence)
and knowing it's God we have to thank
for the Ayatollahs in all our lands
who took us to task, to our senses at last,
with the barrel of Mao's empowering gun
shooting solid silver bullets
up our politically corrected, collective, artistic
bum.

THE EXTREMIST

Based on the principle
that charity begins alone
gently
he ceased hating himself

Time was running in
a constant companion
it seemed to work

The more he used it
the further it took him;
not only, nor even,
to preferred destinations
but usually
               to an equitable
climate of interest   often
to revelation   always
to beckoning   horizons
fresh planted   opportunities
to occasionally sign his name

or marvel
at a passing collection
of dust

A BRIDGE TO PA

(1)

Consider: There are no natural phenomena
less beautiful
than any human manufacture

but we have our moments

one of which I missed on first acquaintance
total lack of Sherlock   well,
you don't expect to find "Breathtaking"
in a face like Pontypridd

(2)

But after sex or poetry
you tend to look around, in fact
I nearly crashed the car
The Staircase Bridge is a bloody marvel

Stone and sinew   Sinew and stone
with fragile imperatives flowing by
Free range this bridge   inspiring listening to it's views
on mind expanded techno-humans
(saved our classic first resort: to Calvary
out of sheer embarrassment).

(3)

In Pontypridd, this local tongue is ill received.
In Venice they'd invest in crumbling

civic pride protect the wonder
full from crass proximities
(if only for the tourist trade)

In Ponty
there's a multi-shame-old-vapid-storey-car-park
and a cop shop, assuming imposition,
by this memory of what we must become.

Built like bouncers at the disco
Fit for adult conversations
between foreheads, noses, cheeks
and fists in ready made bow ties
These buildings have no necks
These buildings have a ring with edges
bright and sharp on every finger (slabs
tattooed with "love" and "hate"
they'll gladly delve, debate with you
the meaning of existence, quoting,
    "*Our* validity
    can beat the sensibility
    out of *your* validity, any
    affray of the year".

(4)

While times removed,
a distant cousin, sullen,
inches from the old,
The New Bridge
(factory farmed on steroids)
doesn't say much
Now and then a mumbled, "Four wheels good
but sixteen's better", and,
"I just do my job, ya know?"

And yards down stream, the chapel,
meek, no hope in hell of inheritance,
is shuffling it's formulae;
the river's steady faith ignored
in favour of a tempting invitation
(formal dress of course: it's times like these
that one regrets The Reformation).

An invite to some high, society celebrations
Topping out with burghers, architects and wives
    eating: salmon mayonnaise
drinking: medium dry white lies
               about progress and prosperity
               prosperity and progress
               while brutality as ever
               takes the fun and only prize

               No wonder this pretending
               to knowledge of another life
               where the boot in the balls
               is not the final arbiter.

(5)

But if the pen is
mightier than the sword
why didn't God
send the Gomorrahns
and Sodomites
a stiffly worded memo?

No.
As ever
these are
and those were

the days of a God who watches
too much television
and can't tell the difference between real
and simulated violence.
So
as ever
these are the days of madmen in sober suits
breaking a better world for their children.

(6)

Fortunately, they are the cure for their own disease
as we   wait...

Must we wait...?

With irritating regularity
and, irritatingly, insufficient irritation
for the temporary relief afforded by wave power.

Perhaps, if we all spat,
or better still
pissed in their predilection
we might erase their scribbles
permanently from the sand,
'though, of course,
we'd have to find somewhere else
to sunbathe.

(7)

"Still", as I heard an able wheelie say,
referring to his paraplegic childhood,
"You can't be unhappy all the time".

                And there
           in The Basin
        at Coasters Retreat
     Kurringai Chase
I found Good News
on a eucalyptus tree;
Written in exotic
script from the roots of existence
and being human
I *knew*
this despatch was meant for *me*
exclusively

'Til the sense in me laughed out loud, remembering
the feeding trail of the worm on it's way to the moth
with the message   "I came   I saw   I ate."

It's all so different when you read it in the original.

(8)

Some say
"You can't go back"

Most people
never leave

I parked
under neon
lights hanging their heads
embarrassed by the new
the hunter's moon
and introduced myself (pilgrim
in search of "real")
and "real", of course, was strewn
with poly-junk-can-arsefood-litter.

          Don't get me wrong,
in The Tate or Metropolitan
this dirt from trite us would have had *depth*
important things to say about *everything*

but on The Staircase Bridge
it was inappropriate
even though "Breathtaking" had stepped out
leaving a dream if ever boned with stone,
now ill-fitted in cracked, unkempt with weeds extruding,
concrete
and an unkind   kind of pebble dash.

(9)

Sinew and stone   Portable phone
Stone and sinew   "We'll get right back to you"
The parapets needed   Orthodontal care
I wandered   To the riverside
Fragile imperatives flowing by

as when the old man
died
and they laid him out
as I'd often wanted to
(tackled him once and he hit
the floor so hard, surprised
he didn't hit back
Lucky I was).

They laid him out
            the hospital did
down in the bowels
            after taking out his
and Mum she asked us
            if we wanted to see
and my brother said no
            because of his reasons

and I said yes
           because of mine
and there he was
                suspended

magicians assistant draped
in a sheet of white
face only visible
my fathers old residence
a soon to be nun.

(10)

Likewise, I was vacant awhile
then touched his cheek with the back of my hand
echo of his
stunning accuracy.

And he.
        Was soft.
And his skin.
        Was perfect.
And I
dismembering all those years
of shared   blood   shed,
was ambushed,
by the loss
of all we'd missed
on first   to last
acquaintance,
total lack of Sherlock   well,
you *shouldn't* expect to find "Breathtaking"
in a face like Pontypridd.

~~~~~~~~~~~~~~~~~~~~~~~

William Edwards 1750
repaired by
Edward David and
Thomas Evan 1798

~~~~~~~~~~~~~~~~~~~~~~~